PEACE

PEACE

سلام שלום

Preface by Chaim Herzog

Text by Anthony S. Pitch

Drawings by Igael Tumarkin

 PUBLISHING, INC.

Introduction

In a world prone to sudden, radical political upheavals whose repercussions extend far beyond the borders of any one state, we have come to place a very high premium upon the virtue of stability. The irony, of course, is that in their craving for stability nations, like individuals, can sometimes grow resigned to even admittedly unpalatable political situations and find themselves falling into line with the kind of thinking that cautions: "Better the devil you know than the devil you don't." In the case of the Middle East, by the latter half of the 1970s the status quo of "no war, no peace"—essentially an imprecise and somewhat cosmetic version of what was in fact "sometimes war but never peace"—had begun to become something of a comfortably familiar situation, while peace had taken on the quality of a vague metaphor that seemed about as realistic and attainable as the vision of the "End of Days."

Israel and her neighbors had been locked in a pattern of negative expectations for so long that only a uniquely dramatic step could have broken its hold over them. President Sadat's declaration that he would go even to Jerusalem in the pursuit of peace, and Prime Minister Begin's invitation to him to do so, was precisely the kind of jolt necessary to startle the Middle East out of its sense of easy familiarity with the status quo. No other move or stage in the subsequent months of negotiations ever matched those opening days of the peace initiative for sheer drama and emotion. Yet even such "shock treatment" would have had only limited therapeutic effect had it not been followed by a period in which both sides had an opportunity to examine and revise many of their firmly imbedded assumptions about themselves and each other. When President Sadat offered to go to Jerusalem and Prime Minister Begin reciprocated with an invitation, the governments of both countries could well afford to enter into the peace venture by calculating their fallback positions and asking themselves philosophically "What have we got to lose?" During the succeeding rounds of negotiations, however, both sides were forced to alter their outlook and seriously begin to consider the far more complex yet enticing prospect of what they had to gain.

It is the pragmatic aspects of this question that now preoccupy not only the political leaders but the citizens of both Egypt and Israel, for ultimately it will be the peoples of these two countries who will forge the content of peace. Unlike the past, however, the benefits of peace are no longer merely a matter for speculation. Much to the contrary, each side must define for itself, in the most concrete terms, exactly what it wants to derive from peace and then establish the means to attain its objectives. The signing of the peace treaty between Egypt and Israel in March 1979 was not the culmination of a process but merely the close of the first stage. In political terms, it marked the formal end to the state of war, but even more important, perhaps, it signalled a shift in the two countries' approach toward the peace process from an experiment to a commitment. Now Egypt and Israel must set about the functional task of *making* peace – in the most literal sense of that word—and thereafter of making peace *work*.

In essence, we have been challenged to prove to the other countries of the region that peace is both viable and valuable, and given the store of enmity and cynicism that has been allowed to fester in the Middle East for so long, that is a formidable assignment. Yet even before the euphoria generated by the peace treaty subsided, both parties to the agreement were keenly aware of the risks and pitfalls involved in such an endeavor. The constitution of peace will require us to draw upon untapped reserves of patience, imagination, and faith in ourselves. We must learn how to trust one another and chart a course that takes into account the need for both stability and flexibility. We will have to develop new perspectives on our weaknesses and strengths and, no less important, on the mistakes and setbacks we will inevitably suffer along the way. The real challenge that peace has placed before all the nations of the Middle East is whether we have the courage to change—gradually, subtly perhaps, but nonetheless fundamentally. I believe that rising to meet that challenge will be a liberating and rehabilitation experience for all who take part in it.

Chaim Herzog

July 1979

Herzliah, Israel

Production: Arye Ben-David
Design: Doreet Scharfstein

ISBN 0-89961-001-3

Photographs: Photograph department, Government Press office by the photographers Moshe Milner, Yaacov Saar and Hananya Hennan.
Photographs on pages 21, 42-3, 47, 138-139 Micha Bar-Am; 16-17, 149 Menucha Brafman; 22, 70-71 Werner Braun; 129 Elliot Faye; 18-19 Igal Havilio; 74-75 Peter Larsen; 13 Aliza Orbach; 24 Yael Rosen; 14-15, 54-55, 66-67 David Rubinger; 20 Yehoshua Zamir. Photograph on p. 137, 148 by Su en lee (Butch) courtesy of Dubek Cigarettes Company and Ariely advertising agency Tel-Aviv.

Nation at War

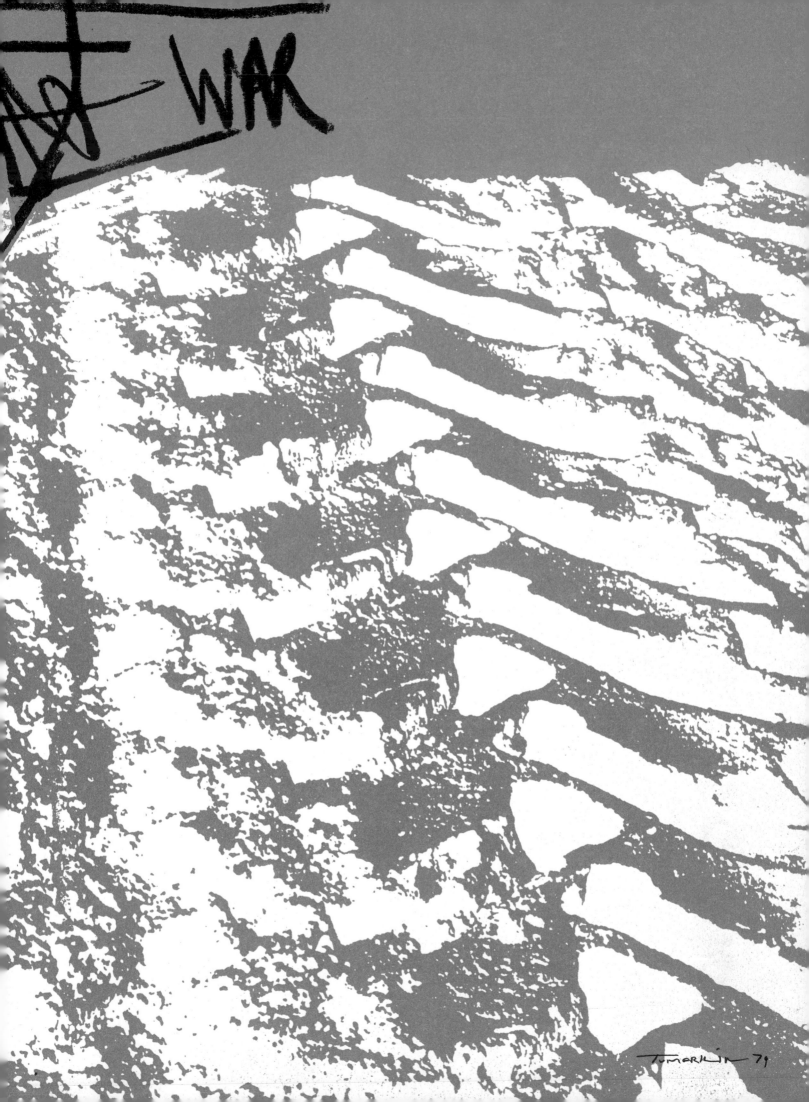

Taking leave of loved ones

Uzi at the ready in all weather

Head down, periscope up

The "trampiada" — where Israel's soldiers "tramp" (hitch) rides to and from military bases

Broad shoulders balance a threat to the man's hopes

Brief visits leave lasting memories

The supreme sacrifice
will never be forgotten

Daddy's home!

The relief of survival

The Long March
From Kilometer 101

THE LONG MARCH FROM KILOMETER 101

As western world leaders assembled at cenotaphs to mark World War Armistice Day an Israeli Major-General and an Egyptian Lieutenant-General saluted each other at the sandy wastes of kilometer 101 on the Suez-Cairo road. Then they sat opposite each other in a tent and a Finnish General from the United Nations broke the silence. "Gentlemen," he said, "let's sign."

After the brief formalities Maj.-Gen. Aharon Yariv, formerly chief of Israel's military intelligence, stepped out jauntily to meet newsmen from around the world. Wearing dark eyeglasses against the mid-afternoon desert sun he told them the agreement just signed represented "the first step on the long road to peace."

But it was a prophecy which fell on deaf, or at best skeptical ears far across the Canal waters in Israel. There, a stunned nation, still reeling from the surprise attack on the Egyptian and Syrian fronts a mere 37 days earlier, grudgingly accepted this cease-fire agreement because it guaranteed the return of some 230 prisoners of war. But it didn't quell the rage they harbored at having their hands tied by the superpowers when poised to smash the encircled Egyptian Third Army. Despondent and wan in mourning for her more than 2500 war dead, Israel now turned viciously on herself in a reckless search for scapegoats. Even the generals publicly accused each other of shortcomings. In this post-war ferment thoughts of peace were furthest from the minds of a population which would accept only months later that its heady victory in the Six Day War had lulled its instincts and dissipated its prowess.

In Egypt euphoria reigned. Whole divisions had swept across the canal and overwhelmed the 436 Israelis manning the bunkered Bar-Lev line. Egyptian troops screaming "Allah Akbar" (Allah is great) had defiantly planted their flag on the reconquered sands of Sinai. In the flush of achieving total surprise over such an agile adversary, President Sadat had in one fell swoop erased the shame of the Egyptian rout of 1967. No matter that the Israelis had rallied magnificently. The U.N. imposed cease-fire had left the Egyptian leader with his Sinai bridgehead intact, begging political movement from the provocative past and the untenable present.

The implacable foes had good reason to court mediation by the formidable U.S. Secretary of State, Henry Kissinger. Egypt had seen him demonstrate his leverage over Israel by quashing plans for the destruction of the Third Army and by playing a key role in airlifting desperately needed supplies during the war. Israel, with her long-standing special relationship with the U.S., could turn nowhere else. Kissinger saw the immediate task as separating the sandwiched armies. But when he convened a peace conference of the embattled nations at Geneva he had a grander vision of the future. Post-war visits to the Middle East had convinced him that no further proof of heroism was necessary. No military point remained to be made. Both sides sought peace. Egypt, he said, sought the recovery of sovereignty and the redress of grievances of a displaced people. Israel sought security and recognition of its legitimacy as a nation. "The common goal of peace," concluded the most powerful U.S. Secretary of State in almost two decades, "must surely be broad enough to embrace all these aspirations."

They sat in the ornately-furnished, marble-walled Palais des Nations on the shores of Lac Leman and while surrounded by murals depicting Justice and Peace, they pored over maps and tackled the disengagement of their forces. Simultaneously, Nobel Peace Prize winner Kissinger visited Middle Eastern capitals to prod, cajole and reason with those who would have to accept the accord. It was a new brand of personal diplomacy in which the former Harvard professor displayed great depth of detail, firm realities about the limits of options, and a flair for winning a minimum measure of trust. Acerbic and often obscene criticism greeted this fellow Jew in democratically vocal Israel and security around him was tight. But consensus was reached in less than a month. Israeli forces would withdraw across pontoon bridges into the Sinai desert, beyond a United Nations buffer zone separating them from the Egyptian bridgehead, and the Egyptians would prepare the Suez Canal for reopening.

A world blackmailed by selective oil embargoes welcomed the outcome with relief. Israel's foremost military analyst, Chaim Herzog, lauded the German-born American for having averted an inevitable new round of hostilities. With great prescience of mind Herzog commented that Sadat's apparent realism and power of decision gave many people in Israel a feeling of hope that perhaps an advance could be made towards peace.

Once again the generals — this time both chiefs of staff — converged on the mustard-colored tent at kilometer 101. Lt.-Gen. Mohammed Gamasy stepped out of a black American limousine with a holstered pistol strapped to his belt while Lt.-Gen. David Elazar alighted from a Bell helicopter, bracing himself against the chill winter winds. When the midday signing of the agreement to disengage troops was over, Elazar pledged his army would not withdraw with a scorched earth policy;

Israel wanted civilian life restored to the devastated Canal area to give Egypt a vested interest in keeping the peace.

While Sadat's stock soared in the land of the pyramids, Israeli leadership limped to a standstill. General elections had returned to power a coalition regarded as the lesser of two evils but it was hard put to withstand the full fury of an aroused public and disarray within the coalition. Protest movements mushroomed, with yesterday's idols becoming today's pariahs. The nation had not balked at sacrifice; now it charged those in power with gross, if not criminal negligence, and demanded retribution. But bereft of policy and lacking credibility, a callous leadership, in the interests of preserving party unity, would not meet demands for even token ministerial sacrifices. It was a time of profound national anguish and political paralysis.

Catharsis came from a time-bomb ticking away ever since a judiciary enquiry commission had been charged with finding out how and why Israel had been surprised by war. Chaired by Supreme Court President Shimon Agranat, the interim report published at the beginning of April became an overnight bestseller, rocked the pillars of Israeli leadership and indicted, by way of innuendo, an entire people for having lived in a fool's paradise in the preceding years. There were charges of the military's blind belief in preconceptions and refusal to budge from preconceived evaluations of the very ability of the Arab neighbors to wage war against Israel. Among those whose resignations were called for were the chief of staff and the head of military intelligence.

The guillotine fell on Elazar, who had stated a mere three days earlier that "the chances are, one day someone in Egypt will decide it is a good thing that they are no longer at war with the Jews." He would not live to see that day. Twenty-four months later, while swimming at a pool near his Tel Aviv home, he was stricken with a heart attack and died within hours.

In a flurry of action to forestall its downfall, the government toyed with reshuffling portfolios within its own ranks, while demanding that Defense Minister Moshe Dayan be sacked. When Dayan refused to bow out unless his colleagues followed suit in a show of collective responsibility, weary septuagenarian Premier Golda Meir brought down the government with her own resignation. But symptomatic of a party fossilized in power, the party bosses refused to go to the country, preferring to pick a new leader whose presence evoked the glorious days of June 1967. They chose Yitzhak Rabin, chief of staff during the Six Day War.

It took almost two months for the newcomer to stitch together a viable government, during which time Israeli and Syrian frontline troops pounded each other with an almost daily barrage of whining shells. Kissinger took up the political slack by extracting a list of Israeli prisoners of war held in Damascus, then plunging into 32 days of rigorous shuttling between the capitals. The Middle East had never seen such flamboyant tenacity of purpose during which the rotund professor brushed aside taunts of being a traitor against his own people. When agreement was finally reached there were dividends for both camps. Israel's yearning for a return of all prisoners of war would be traded for a withdrawal from vast chunks of overrun Syrian land. As was the case with Egypt, a United Nations force would keep the warriors apart by occupying a buffer zone.

On 1st June 1974 a turbo-jet Fokker aircraft with blue and white U.N. colors taxied to a halt at Ben-Gurion international airport after a direct flight from Damascus. The House of Israel watched television misty-eyed as the first 12 POWs were assisted down to the tarmac for jubilant family reunions. But when the eyes were dry again peace was as elusive as ever and people asked each other — "What now?"

RUMBLING WAR CLOUDS

A Watergate-hounded president in search of applause found it in the streets of Cairo when two million people gave him a tumultuous welcome. Not since 1945 had an American President visited Egypt and his triumphant odyssey would make him the first U.S. chief executive to set foot in Saudi Arabia, Syria, Israel and Jordan.

The June 1974 extravaganza justly crowned American achievement in positioning itself as the Middle East's power broker. The visit, said Kissinger pointedly, was a symbolic affirmation of a dramatic reversal now that the U.S. was beginning a new relationship with all countries in the area. But neither Nixon nor Kissinger expected such laurels on their first stop. Frenzied Cairenes showered rose petals and confetti on the open limousine where both presidents stood waving along the 13 kilometer route from Cairo's international airport to al-Qubbah Palace. The Egyptians, who had only recently restored a seven year break in diplomatic relations, chanted "Nixon, Man of Peace". And a much-boosted Nixon, whose envoy at Nasser's funeral had predicted that Sadat would last only six weeks, expansively praised his host as a man of vision and statesmanship. Yet the American, who was to enjoy the limelight for only two more months before being hounded out of office, soberly cautioned against quick solutions. On a barnstorming train ride through the fertile Nile Delta, with Sadat seated beside him, he said the issues would have to be handled carefully and "not in a melodramatic grandstand play, where everybody cheers then all of it suddenly falls down."

His welcomes were warm but restrained in Saudi Arabia, Syria and Jordan, where he heard the dolorous refrain for a solution to the Palestinian problem. But when Nixon stepped out of his "Spirit of 76" airliner to a 21-gun salute at Ben-Gurion international airport, the Israeli President paid him public homage for standing by Israel "in hours of grave peril and in days of opportunity and hope." Nixon replied that when he last visited Israel at the end of the Six Day War peace had seemed an impossible dream. Now it was a possibility. Later, at a Knesset banquet, as he stood below Marc Chagall's wall tapestry of Moses holding the Ten Commandments, Nixon tempered wild hopes with searing realism. Building peace in the Middle East would be more difficult than ending the Vietnam War, more difficult than the U.S. opening to China, and more difficult than continuing the dialogue between the superpowers. But "initiatives might lead to negotiation".

If further proof were needed of the new assertive American role it came bluntly from Kissinger, who stood almost alone in his conviction that the Arab states had come to accept the existence of the State of Israel. The hardened pattern of the American-Israel alliance facing the Soviet-Arab alignment was breaking down, giving way to a more complex relationship, with the U.S. now befriending both sides.

With American prestige at a peak, Arab ministers followed each other in quick succession on the political pilgrimage to Washington. Not even Nixon's exit in disgrace could change the new reality. The real architect of America's new "even-handed" policies remained firmly ensconced in the State Department.

Yet Israelis began to sound the alarm of imminent war in the tinderbox region. Newly-appointed Chief of Staff Mordechai Gur went so far as to forecast a date — towards the end of summer. Defense Minister Shimon Peres, declaring that "the Arab world now looks to war", felt "compelled to present the harsh truth to the people." And then, for the first time in almost 20 years, Israel's citizen army sped to bases in a nationwide practice call-up.

Every feint, ploy or policy speech seemed to goad the other side like a red cape. The Syrians reined in their civilians wanting to return to the repossessed Golan Heights town of Kuneitra. In Egypt Sadat rumbled ominously about the intolerable state of neither war nor peace. A year after the guns blazed on Yom Kippur, Premier Rabin recited the new fundamental creed that Israel would under no circumstances return all of the captured Sinai desert. The Egyptian response came from the Minister of War: Sinai would return to Egypt — whether by peace or by war. In this tremulous calm a kibbutznik counseled further talks. "Now is the best chance to get a political settlement," said Foreign Minister Yigal Alon. "War is behind us and the fear of another war is in front of us."

It was a forlorn expectation. An Arab summit in Rabat, Morocco, proclaimed the Palestine Liberation Organization (PLO) as the sole legitimate representative of the Palestinians. The effect was as if the summiteers had raised a spiked head on the highway to peace. Nothing could more effectively have doomed any accommodation with Israel. Nothing united Israelis more than their implacable hatred of the PLO, which spawned massacre of the innocents and which was committed by its own covenant to the destruction of the renascent Jewish state.

Topping this setback was Israel's growing isolation by a world community cowed by terror and the post-war oil weapon. Only two weeks after the Rabat summit, PLO leader Yasser Arafat swaggered up to the rostrum of the United Nations General Assembly, a pistol holster swinging by his side, and roundly flayed Israel as a racist, reactionary and colonialist state. Israel watched the spectacle with loathing which turned to outrage six days later after a PLO gang infiltrated a Jordan Valley frontier town and butchered four Israelis before being gunned down themselves.

Jitters touched the guardians of peace on both sides of the borders. Syria declared a military state of alert, only to be faced by a partially-mobilized Hebrew-speaking army. Israel's Major-General Ariel Sharon — who had led the Jewish state's counter-thrust across the Suez Canal — thundered his reasons for resigning his Knesset seat to be eligible for the army reserves: "We are facing the prospects of a harsh war that may well be decisive for the survival of the state."

Another round of step-by-step diplomacy was imperative. The alternative, thought Premier Rabin, would mean an unwieldly re-run of the Geneva Conference and with it the war option. President Ford went further in picturing "a high likelihood of war."

While the fragile peace held on the frontiers it collapsed on the domestic scene. The aftermath of war had stretched the economies of both Egypt and Israel to the periphery of endurance and workers in Cairo and Tel Aviv took to the streets in violent rioting and looting to protest price hikes and low wages. Peace, then, was a daunting aspiration as the new calendar year dawned. But in the shadow of the biblical city of Hebron opposition leader Menachem Begin paused during an address to his party's convention to talk of shalom and salaam to visiting Egyptian journalist Sana Hassan. "Tell your people," he said, "that Jewish soldiers have mothers who hate war just as Arab mothers do, and that the Jewish People loves peace and respects its Arab neighbors."

THE MAGICIAN RETURNS

Buckling under the financial strain of digging new frontier defenses in the desert, Israel felt checkmated at every turn, knowing that all the improvements would pass to the Egyptian army after a second withdrawal. The tottering economy, devalued by 42 per cent, could barely take the strain of beefing up the Sinai to the tune of IL. 400 million, with another IL. 1 billion set aside to complete the program. The crunch came when pressures mounted for an Israeli handover of the Gulf of Suez oilfields — gushing $1 million of oil a day — and the vital Mitla and Gidi passes, through which an invader had to enter to overrun the desert.

As Kissinger flew into Cairo to a familiarly warm embrace from Sadat it was clear that the options had narrowed. A bid for overall peace at a Geneva conference would be stillborn. The step-by-step approach at least provided visible proof of some conquered lands changing hands for political concessions, though the parties skirted the Palestinian minefield.

Kissinger shuttled between the enemy tents with characteristic verve, forever a pulse-beat ahead of his weary entourage, popping up like a jack-in-the-box to outwit scornful critics, and worrying the politicians out of their Levantine lethargy and captive ideologies. But his virtuoso performance fell flat at the end of several weeks when Israel stonewalled on her demand for a non-belligerency pact.

On his return home he reported to U.S. Senators that there was now a greater danger of an Arab-Israeli war and the world shifted uneasily. But attention focused fortuitously beyond Israel's northern border where a bloody civil war burst open in Lebanon, sucking the Arab world into its vortex and crumpling all pretence of Arab unity. Israel, forever suspicious that the Jewish Secretary of State would lean over backwards to accommodate the Arabs, felt somewhat vindicated in standing up to Kissinger's recent overtures; his Asian peace pact lay in tatters as the Vietcong overran South Vietnam and Israel was going to have none of a similar kind of peace.

The Egyptian maverick was the first to try and break the stalemate. When he met the American President in neutral Austria, Sadat put out feelers on the possibility of U.S. personnel manning early-warning stations in the Sinai passes to prevent surprise attack by either side. Israel's unilateral gesture of goodwill was to thin her forces on the Suez front as the Egyptians cleared the last war debris from the canal. The theatrical opening of the 100 kilometer waterway was conducted with great flourish amid world-wide publicity. As loudspeakers hailed the hero of the canal crossing and warplanes dipped in salute overhead, Sadat arrived resplendent in the dress whites of an admiral to a booming 21-gun salute and a fanfare of trumpets. Then he boarded a destroyer to lead a convoy of vessels majestically south from Port Said to Ismailiya. With almost a quarter of a million civilians resettled in the canal zone's war-battered towns, and a vulnerable Europe now closer to the vast Arabian oilfields, Sadat justifiably hailed the reopening as "a contribution to peace".

But Nasser's heir could not rid himself of a credibility gap. No sooner had he told a BBC TV 'Panorama' team that "the main lesson to be learned from the October War is that the Arab-Israeli conflict will never be solved by war," than he warned of war if diplomacy failed. And only at the eleventh hour did this former army colonel, who had seized the Cairo radio station in 1952 to broadcast news of the army coup, draw back from his ultimatum to block U.N. troops from remaining in the sensitive buffer zone. He again turned his cheek on face to face talks with Israeli leaders, telling the visiting Mexican President that he could not negotiate while his lands were still occupied.

A restless Kissinger continued to jab a distrustful Israel to "take a chance on making progress towards peace." On the eve of yet another of his flights to the volatile crossroads of Africa and Asia, impassioned crowds outside Israel's parliament building shrieked against submitting to U.S. dictates. Inside the raucous chamber opposition leader Menachem Begin charged the government with surrender by stages. A Yom Kippur War hero demonstratively returned his country's highest award for bravery to protest what he called the government's capitulation. And when Kissinger touched down in Israel, supporters of Gush Emunim — the movement rabidly opposed to Jewish withdrawal from biblically sanctified Judea and Samaria — pelted cabinet ministers with eggs and blocked the coastal road entrance to Jerusalem. Though shrill, the outbursts were in vain as the 12-day shuttle climaxed with agreement in both Cairo and Jerusalem. An ebullient Kissinger hoped it would be remembered as the point when peace began. Egypt had won back the oilfields and the passes in return for a written pledge that "the conflict would not be resolved by military force but by peaceful means." Also conceded by Egypt was the right of passage through the Suez Canal of non-military cargoes to and from Israel, and a promise not to blockade the Jewish state. Both sides, and the Americans, would have early-warning stations in the Sinai passes, there would be a limited forces zone, the agreement would remain in force until superseded by another and the parties agreed to strive for a negotiated peace.

As Israel's Chief of Staff signed the accord on 1st September 1975 he remarked, "I'll only know in another five years whether I did a good thing." When the Soviets boycotted the formal signing in Geneva, the Egyptian President charged them with open incitement against his country. But this did not signal any closer affection between the two signatories in the Palais des Nations. There were neither handshakes, greetings nor even speeches. It was all over in 11 minutes.

Weeks later Sadat became the first Egyptian leader to pay a state visit to Washington where an honor guard awaited him on the White House lawn and an effusive President Ford praised him for his sincerity, moderation and wisdom. The Egyptians had been successfully weaned from the Soviet bosom and Israel took anxious note of the new realities. Despite his controversial anti-Zionist remarks before the National Press Club, Sadat enjoyed a blaze of goodwill, more so when a Greek freighter bound with Rumanian cement for Eilat became the first ship in 23 years to carry cargo to Israel through the Suez Canal. At the end of his 10-day pageant he was given a standing ovation by a joint meeting of Congress. "Our desire to establish peace is our paramount consideration and overriding concern," he told the U.S. legislators. "We are paving the road to peace even if this entails taking some risks," intoned the President of Egypt as Capitol Hill resounded with applause.

A NEW BROOM

Smouldering passions over rival claims to Holy Land had lain dormant while the offspring of Isaac and Ishmael crawled away from open conflict. Wellwishers egged them on to bury the past and build for the future. But suddenly the foundations for peace were rocked by vitriolic

Jew-baiting at the United Nations. Egypt voted with an overwhelming majority that "Zionism is a form of racism and racial discrimination". The vote splashed like sulphuric acid on the hands of those Israelis trying to scale the wall of suspicion. And it gave succour to partisans bellowing that Israel had won the wars but was losing the peace. The vote had touched the nerve center of all Israelis of goodwill, to whom Zionism was a national liberation movement, freeing Jews from 2000 years of persecution in exile and returning them to their land, where they were once again a free and independent people.

However, for almost a year afterwards all the parties were involved in holding operations. While Egypt and Israel consolidated along their new lines, Syria became embroiled in the Lebanese conflagration, invading with 30,000 troops to try and impose a Pax Syriana. A U.S. election year saw presidential contenders and congressional aspirants vying with each other to woo the Jewish lobby and sing the praises of Israel. With the U.S. and Israel working once more in tandem, calls by Egypt and the Soviet Union for a resumption of the Geneva conference, with the PLO participating as an equal partner, were quickly rebuffed. As time went by a feeling gained ground that the problem was insoluble and when Premier Rabin said the struggle could last for two or three generations he voiced the inner feelings of many people of different creeds and cultures.

The election of an inexperienced Democratic standard-bearer to the presidency of the United States coincided with an erosion of power in both the Egyptian and Israeli governments. In authoritarian Egypt the bloodiest street battles since the monarchy was toppled broke out between disenchanted workers and the authorities. Rioters in Cairo and Alexandria were slain while violently protesting more price rises and the removal of many subsidies. The government, while quick to charge the communists with plotting its overthrow, just as swiftly revoked some of the price hikes. But there was anxiety abroad as no Egyptian government, if it survived, could be seen to be making concessions to Israel from a weakened power base.

In Israel, the dominant Labor Party which had ruled without interruption for 29 years, swayed amid scandal and corruption. One after the other party stalwarts holding the highest positions of public trust were arraigned and convicted of theft, fraud, bribery and tax evasion. And although the country was passing through lean and austere times, it lurched from one economically ruinous strike to another. With his party wracked by power struggles, Premier Rabin sacked a coalition party for abstaining on a no-confidence motion and then called a general election to forestall his own certain parliamentary defeat. In the interim, he too was caught in the web of scandal and resigned as party leader after admitting to keeping an illegal foreign currency account abroad. When polling booths closed forecasts were that the ruling party would be returned with a shaven majority. However, a post-midnight tally had cameramen racing round to Likud Party leader Menachem Begin's headquarters. To the surprise even of his campaign manager, Begin had romped home after a 29-year deep freeze.

His thaw was not long in coming. A day later he stood among religious mystics in a West Bank army camp where the outgoing government housed them after thwarting attempts at illegal settlement in a place called Eilon Moreh. Proclaiming there would be many more Eilon Morehs within weeks or months, Menachem Begin chilled friend and foe alike by tagging the occupied lands "liberated territories". Then he chided reporters who asked if he would annex the West Bank: "You annex foreign land, not your own country," said the man who had a price of $10,000 on his head while leading the underground Irgun Zvai Leumi during the British Mandate.

The new Israeli Prime Minister shared much in common with the Egyptian leader across the Nile. Both were patriots steeled by early horrors: Sadat's daughter had died of malnutrition during his imprisonment; Begin's parents had perished at the hands of the Nazis and he himself had been imprisoned by the Russians. Both had been implacable foes of the British colonial presence in their own countries. The Jew had gone underground to lead an armed Hebrew revolt against the occupation forces. The Arab had made contact with Nazi spies and been jailed in the process. Courteous and cultured linguists, both were humble before their common God. The Egyptian drew inspiration from frequent visits to his Nile Delta village birthplace. The Israeli continued to live modestly in his Tel Aviv apartment. The president and the premier shared consummate political skills, deftly swaying crowds with emotive rhetoric, spellbinding oratory, more than a touch of showmanship and an innate belief that they encompassed the fate of their peoples. They revelled in walking the stage of contemporary history and both had, within a short time of acceding to power, reached the stature of their predecessors. Wielding unchallenged power by mid-1977, both Begin and Sadat were impelled by verbal commitment to imminent collision. Each made clear that he would not yield an inch of land to the other. A showdown even loomed with Israel's indispensable ally as the new American President called for a homeland for the Palestinians. The Likud government's answer came from war hero General Sharon, now in charge of settlement policy, when he outlined a 20 year plan for settling two million Jews from the Golan Heights to Sharm el Sheikh. Begin himself rejected any talks with the PLO, whose philosophy he disdainfully described as based on an Arabic Mein Kampf.

A bemused world snickered when Begin announced his proposed draft treaty with Egypt would be discussed with Washington. However, ears pricked up when unconfirmed reports headlined secret meetings in North Africa between new Israeli Foreign Minister, Moshe Dayan, and Arab leaders. This was soon dismissed as the gimmick of an untried government and events slid back into the familiar thrust and parry of Middle East fencing. In October Sadat threatened war, to which Begin replied: "All wars between us and you ended with your defeat." The knives were being unsheathed and sharpened for what would be the fifth Arab-Israeli war and the third to break out in October.

Discussing deployment
of troops at kilometer 101

Finnish General Ensio Silasvuo of the United Nations, arrives for talks with Egyptian and Israeli generals in the sandy desert wastes

opposite: Lieutenant-General David Elazar, Chief of Staff of the Israel Defense Forces, straightens his beret after signing the agreement at kilometer 101 to withdraw his troops across the Suez Canal

(above) United Nations soldier on guard duty at kilometer 101
(below) Egyptian guard duty troops at the signing of the cease-fire agreement

Dr. Henry Kissinger, architect of the step-by-step approach to peace, master of shuttle diplomacy and the most powerful U.S. Secretary of State in almost two decades

(above) The awesome peaks of the Sinai mountains
(left) Taking up new positions after the cease-fire agreement
(right) United Nations troops kept the warring sides apart

Israel's former chief of military intelligence,
Major-General Aharon Yariv,
waves to newsmen after signing the
cease-fire agreement at kilometer 101
on the Suez-Cairo road

(top left) Israeli Chief of Staff, Lt. Gen. David Elazar (left) emerges from the mustard-colored tent at kilometer 101 after signing the agreement to withdraw across the Suez Canal with his opposite number, Lt.-Gen. Mohammed Gamasy (center)

(top center) Last chance for a dip in Egyptian waters before withdrawing into the desert

(bottom) Israeli soldiers enjoy a game of shesh-besh while the generals and the politicians wrangle in the aftermath of war

The Suez Canal reopens to shipping after an eight-year closure

(left) Folding the tents and rolling the bedding for relocation east of the Suez Canal
(right) The Israeli flag is borne away from a Canal zone city

Jubilation as the trucks carry Israeli soldiers home to demobilization

The war is over. The cease-fire is signed. The troops are separated by neutral United Nations forces. Now there is time to sing again and to resume work and be reunited with the children

President Richard Nixon speaks at a banquet in Israel's Knesset.

Sadat in Jerusalem

On the same day that Israeli warplanes zeroed in on terrorist bases in Lebanon to avenge civilians slain in a Galilean town, President Sadat was changing the course of history. He electrified Egyptian parliamentarians with a bold challenge: "I am ready to go to the end of the world to get a settlement. I am even ready to go to Israel, to the Knesset, and speak to all the members of the Israeli parliament there and negotiate with them over a peace settlement." To thunderous applause, the man who had stepped into Nasser's shoes a bare seven years earlier, added: "The Israelis are going to be stunned when they hear that I am ready to meet them in their home."

But Sadat's political swerve was greeted with skepticism bordering on derision in Israel. A leopard didn't change its spots and Israelis had grown wary of dramatic reversals in the breast-beating tradition of the Middle East. Begin was politely circumspect, retorting that if it was not just rhetoric and Sadat was really prepared to come to the Knesset, he welcomed this willingness. However, that same day the Israeli Premier told visiting U.S. congressmen departing for Egypt that Sadat would be welcomed with all honor and full ceremony if his intentions of coming were genuine. A day later Begin broke new ground, appearing to upstage Sadat with a radio and TV broadcast to the Egyptian public, in which he urged "no more wars, no more bloodshed."

Observers chuckled as these two nationalists played cat and mouse. Sadat told CBS anchorman Walter Cronkite that he would visit Jerusalem within a week of receiving a formal invitation. The same evening Begin told visiting Canadian Zionists of his readiness to dispatch a written invitation if the Egyptian President was "really ready to come to Jerusalem". The next day Begin put his promise into writing, beginning his 314 word letter with the words, "Dear Mr. President, on behalf of the Government of Israel I have the honor to extend to you our cordial invitation to come to Jerusalem and to visit our country." The formal letter, delivered via U.S. diplomats in Israel and Egypt, concluded with Begin assuring the Egyptian "that the Parliament, the Government and the people of Israel, will receive you with respect and cordiality."

Incredulity persisted when Israel's Chief of Staff was recalled from abroad and publicly rapped on the knuckles for stating in a newspaper interview that Sadat might be maneuvering to pull the wool over the country's eyes and that Israel knew the Egyptian army was then at the height of preparing for war.

With dazzling rapidity both countries announced the visit would materialize in two days and when, with one day to go, a planeload of

Egyptians, led by the head of the Presidential Bureau, landed in Israel to finalize arrangements, it finally dawned on everyone that the countries had moved from fantasy to the brink of historical drama.

A captive TV audience around the world watched the presidential Boeing 737 of the Arab Republic of Egypt drone out of the night sky and roar down the runway, taxiing to a stop before a red carpet at 8 p.m. on Saturday, 19th November 1977. Hushed and expectant, the world caught its breath in a way it had not done since Neil Armstrong left the first footprint on the moon. As Israelis sat bunched around TV sets and whispered "Ani lo ma'amin" (I don't believe it), Sadat and Begin stood to attention side by side when the two national anthems were played and a 21-gun salute boomed in honor of the visitor. Fixed opinions of the past vaporized as the commander of the honor guard saluted the supreme commander of the Egyptian Armed Forces and together they marched over to inspect the contingent from Israel's armed services.

Bewilderment and suspense gave way to gasps of disbelief and gathering excitement as the dignified Egyptian warmly greeted the assembly of erstwhile foes. A generation of ice cracked as the lean Arab joked and bantered. Shaking former Premier Golda Meir's hand with undisguised sincerity he said he had waited a long time to see her. "Mr. President, I too have been waiting a long time to see you," she answered. "Well, here I am!" he said with a broad smile. When greeting General Sharon, who'd led the Israeli crossing of the Suez Canal in the 1973 war, Sadat beamed, "If you attempt to cross again I'll put you in jail!" The bulky soldier replied, "Oh, no! I'm Minister of Agriculture now."

During the following 44 hours Sadat charmed and mesmerized. Doubters became believers. Opponents relished the passing pageant. Men, women and children feasted on a spectacle whose every moment was precious. On the morrow of his flight into the unknown, with an Arab world baying for his blood and an Israeli public saluting his courage, the Egyptian leader prayed at Jerusalem's El Aksa Mosque, outside of which King Abdullah of Jordan had been assassinated within living memory. After his visit to Calvary in the Church of the Holy Sepulchre, the Egyptian walked solemnly around the halls of Yad Vashem — Israel's central memorial to the six million Jewish victims of the Nazi holocaust. His Arabic and English inscriptions in the visitors' book were brief: "May God guide our steps towards peace. Let us end all suffering for mankind."

Sadat played havoc with popular prejudices and preconceptions. Even those who saw him playing a masterly game of poker could not fault his deft shuffling of the cards. Every gesture made history, particularly when the leader of 40 million Egyptians paid homage with bowed head when laying a wreath at the Knesset monument to Israel's fallen soldiers. In the Knesset his restated hard-line was lost in the phenomenal moment of the President of a country in a state of war with Israel addressing her elected leaders in the highest chamber of debate. Sadat again called for an end to the occupation of territories, for the right of the Palestinians to establish their own state, and for a free and open city of Jerusalem. But there was an historic departure from this worn litany. "I come to you today on solid ground to shape a new life and prepare a peace. We welcome you among us, with full security and safety. This in itself is a tremendous turning point. We used to reject you."

Begin, a survivor of Nazi-occupied Europe, reasserted Jewish right to its land, citing the spirit of Israel's proclamation of Independence for validity: "It was in this country that we created our civilization and our prophets had their visions. Here we became a people." Yet he, too, responded with an olive branch by calling for annulment of the state of war and letting "everything be subject to negotiations."

Israelis, who had become so accustomed to bellicose boasts from Sadat and raucous political duels among themselves, sat entranced before live TV to watch lucid, reasoned statements by Knesset political factions who put their cases before Sadat in separate meetings. His studied replies, evading pitfalls and responding in broad generalities warmed them to him. "It must go on, face to face between us and between you," said Golda Meir with Sadat seated beside her, "so that even an old lady like I am will live to see the day — you always called me an old lady," at which point both she and Sadat burst out laughing. "I want to see that day and peace between you and us, and peace between all our neighbors."

The tall Egyptian over and over stressed that his goal in having made the astonishing journey was to break down the barriers of distrust, hatred and separation. When he arrived at Ben-Gurion international airport on Monday afternoon for the return flight home he had cast an image of himself as an eminently reasonable, receptive, urbane, civilized man. Perhaps it had been the guile of a superb politico, but for the moment no one dared consider it for fear that, like Shakespeare's Caliban, they would "cry to dream again". As his plane lifted off for the direct route to Cairo, Premier Begin led airport VIPs in waving an emotional farewell. In a parting gesture for the new era, four

Israeli Kfir warplanes flew in an honor escort beside the departing Boeing.

Events of the past two days had dynamically transformed the course of events. A brave Egyptian had taken a gamble and made himself a prime assassination target for hostile Arabs. But he had answered Israel's consistent plea for direct negotiations and would go down in history as a man who changed the destiny of nations. When he returned to Egypt he sat down to complete the last chapter of his autobiography. "I will stand by my peace initiative," he wrote, "whatever happens."

Seconds after setting foot on Israeli soil, President Sadat and Prime Minister Begin stand to attention while their national anthems are played

The Egyptian leader's historic visit to Jerusalem lasted 44 hours, during which he and the Israeli leader availed themselves of every opportunity to get to know one another better

A courageous Arab acknowledges the applause of the Israel cabinet
(foreground) after inspecting an Israeli guard of
honor at Ben-Gurion international airport

Even when others held the microphone President Anwar Sadat remained the focus of attention. During his ice-breaking visit to Jerusalem he is pictured (left) in the Knesset while Labor Party leader Shimon Peres addresses Israeli legislators (center) in jovial mood flanked by Foreign Minister Moshe Dayan and Premier Menachem Begin at a banquet (right) with earphones plugged in for a simultaneous translation of Begin's speech, while Knesset Speaker Yitzhak Shamir listens attentively

Time and again Sadat declared his goal in flying to Israel had been to break down the barriers of distrust, hatred and separation. He never verred from this course, whether in lighter moments, as with Begin, or in profound discussions (below) with Moshe Dayan.

The day after his arrival in Jerusalem, the devout Egyptian statesman prayed in the 8th century Mosque of El Aksa, accompanied by his entourage and local Moslem religious leaders.

Opposite (Above) President Sadat meets with West Bank notables. (Below) Grandmother Golda Meir talks politics minutes before presenting the Egyptian with a present for his newly-born grandchild. Labor Party chairman Shimon Peres looks on.

(Top) A particularly warm relationship was established between Israeli Defense Minister Ezer Weizman and President Sadat.
(Center) President Ephraim Katzir welcomes the pipe-smoking honored guest to his official residence in Jerusalem. From left, Premier Begin, Mrs. Nina Katzir, President Sadat, President Katzir and Mrs. Aliza Begin.
(Bottom) Newmen from around the world covering one of the major stories of the century.

Deep in prayer in the Mosque of El Aksa, built to commemmorate the prophet Mohammed's night journey from Mecca to Jerusalem. It was at the entrance to this mosque that King Abdullah of Jordan was assassinated by an Arab extremist in 1951.

An historic gesture as the supreme commander of the Egyptian Armed Forces honors Israel's fallen soldiers at a wreath-laying ceremony.

The Hour of Decision

Israelis blinked themselves out of the spell when their one-eyed pragmatic foreign minister announced discomfortingly that "the hour of decision is at hand." But they had hardly begun to consider the bottom line of their concessions when the Egyptian put them into a top-spin with his call to a peace conference in Cairo. It threw the Arab world into turmoil, with five radical countries freezing all ties with Egypt and Sadat retaliating by expelling their diplomats.

While the Soviets spiked their invitation, Israel picked top civil servants for the first meaningful face to face talks since Armistice agreements at Rhodes in 1949. The absence of an agenda and the fact that Sadat had kept delegate representation below cabinet rank was immaterial in this spring of detente. Suddenly there was a whiff of what peace could herald. Israeli reporters swarmed into Egypt and their Hebrew by-lines above the Cairo dateline moved their readers into paroxysms of excitement. Every new report seemed to work like laser beams on the walls of the fortified state.

Three weeks to the day after Sadat's tumultuous return home from Jerusalem, the Israeli delegation flew into Cairo in an El Al Boeing painted with the words Shalom and Salaam, and the flags of the two nations fluttering outside the cockpit. Despite much fanfare, the formal opening at the historic Mena House Hotel near the great pyramids was overshadowed by the surprise flight that same day of the Israeli Prime Minister to the United States. The peace proposals he pocketed were shrouded in secrecy but when he unveiled them to President Carter he got the qualified support he sought. Sadat was sufficiently tempted into immediately inviting Begin for talks in Egypt.

The world was agog at the prospect of an early breakthrough. Peace seemed to be at hand. A buoyant Begin went on nationwide American TV to lift the lid slightly on his plans for autonomy in the West Bank. They would be subject to negotiations but, said Israel's premier for the past seven months, the offer was so good he doubted Sadat could reject it. The new whirlwind diplomacy buffeted the residual defenses of a groggy public, carrying it inexorably forward to new frontiers of normality. Thus, when Defense Minister Ezer Weizman flew into Alexandria for talks with Sadat and War Minister Gamasy, his cautious observations on the forthcoming summit were lost in the titillating novelty of his very presence in Egypt.

The season of goodwill was climaxing for the Christian world as an Israeli airliner cruised along the Mediterranean coast carrying a Jewish Prime Minister for his fateful meeting with a Moslem President. The plane banked over Port Said and clung to the Suez Canal route before the landing gear came out over the Egyptian military airbase at Abu Suwayr, near Ismailiya. Other Israeli planes had swooped over the same runways in 1967 and 1973, unleashing their deadly cargo at the height of war, but now Israel's elected leader stepped out to handshakes from Egyptian cabinet ministers and bouquets from Arab children.

The Christmas Day talks opened at the presidential resthouse on a peninsula jutting into Lake Timsah, and renamed Peace Island for the occasion. An auspicious opening, with Begin wishing Sadat a happy 59th birthday and hoping there would be full peace before the Egyptian leader turned 60, was followed by exacting talks. During a break Sadat took the wheel of his Cadillac to drive Begin and Weizman around the fertile area. At the end of the day's summit both sides hinted at a positive turn. Begin believed there would be "peace as early as in a few months," to which Sadat added, "I fully agree." The Israeli ministers retired to sleep in the spacious villa once owned by canal builder Ferdinand de Lesseps, while officials from both countries worked late into the night over the wording of a joint declaration. But in the morning hopes were dashed with a yawning gap over the future of the West Bank Arabs. Egypt was insistent on a Palestinian state being set up. Israel stood guard over the autonomy plan and the self-rule it envisaged. The two statesmen nimbly side-stepped the Palestinian issue and moved ahead on other fronts by setting up a political committee with foreign ministers to assemble in Jerusalem and a military committee with defense ministers to meet in Cairo.

Even though Begin won overwhelming backing for his peace package in a marathon 11½ hour Knesset debate, there were ominous signs that a new deadlock loomed on the future of the settlements Israel had built over the years in the dry Rafiah salient of the northern Sinai. On New Year's Day 1978 Dayan tried to allay the fears of 3,000 settlers gathered at a showpiece agricultural settlement in the area, telling them that while Egyptian sovereignty would return to the entire desert, Israel's defense forces and civil administration would retain strong links with Israelis who continued to farm there. Simultaneously, Israel rushed earth-moving equipment into the disputed tract to prepare new ground for settlements and to expand existing ones. The settlements, Begin promised with vigor, would not be dismantled.

Peace, which had seemed within grasp on Christmas Day, receded daily. When the military committee met in the ancient Egyptian capital on 11th January the Arabs demanded wholesale evacuation of the Sinai settlements. Sadat accused Israel of wanting land and not security. Impatient at progress and backed by a world chorus for some dramatic gesture from Israel, the Egyptian President lamented publicly that he had received nothing in return for his seven-week-old peace initiative.

Begin responded on the very eve of the opening of the political committee in Jerusalem, by telling visiting U.S. congressmen "any prime minister who gives up the Rafiah area settlements would be thrown out. But I would resign before that." The wounded dove of peace was being exposed daily to more deadly flak. Arabic-speaking Moshe Dayan, who had played a key role in the Armistice agreements with Egypt three decades earlier, warned sonorously "it is better that the Sadat initiative should slip through our fingers than that Israel's security and existence should slip through."

Within 48 hours the Egyptian leader stunned the world and even his own delegates in Jerusalem by recalling them to Cairo and temporarily suspending even the military talks in Cairo. Relations plummeted, with Sadat fulminating in his parliament against Begin's "arrogance and expansionism" and the Egyptian press unleashing a venomous spate of anti-Semitic articles. Active American intervention got the Cairo talks going again but the peace balloon was punctured and fast losing height.

The historic visit to Jerusalem was relegated to the background as terrorists landed on Israel's Mediterranean coast, hijacked a bus and in the ensuing shoot-out left 37 shot dead or incinerated, a move which prompted an Israeli military sweep into Lebanon to occupy a massive chunk of land for 91 days. Swift on the heels of this action the Israeli and U.S. leaders met in Washington, where Begin rebuffed all pleas and pressures to freeze new settlements in the West Bank and to pull out of the Sinai farms. The divisive issue was fertilizing mass rallies in Israel for and against a change of policy, with Begin supporters rallying to the "Secure Peace" barricades and his detractors swelling the ranks of "Peace Now".

After Israel's cabinet dithered and finally replied evasively to U.S. spot questions on the future of the West Bank and its inhabitants, Sadat stood before his troops on the Canal front, telling them he might be forced into a new "battle of liberation". The dapper Israeli confronted his critics head on: "They describe me as a barrier to peace. I am a barrier," he said, "but to surrender."

A meeting of Israeli, Egyptian and U.S. foreign ministers at heavily fortified Leeds Castle in England failed to breathe new life into the deflated hopes and obdurate statements followed thick and fast. Begin curtly refused to give "a single grain of sand" as a gesture of goodwill in return for nothing, while Sadat reacted by shutting the doors of all further talks "until this (statement) is declared cancelled."

August came, and with it the dehydrating Middle Eastern heat. In Washington intelligence reports of a build-up of Egyptian armed forces were rushed to the White House. Fearing that Sadat might launch another war in October, as he later told American news media executives, Carter took the initiative by inviting both Sadat and Begin to a trilateral summit at the Camp David, Maryland presidential retreat. The dramatic summons was fraught with danger. The president had placed his political prestige on the line when the trend of the past eight months gave no cause for optimism. Failure, said the soft-spoken Georgian, could result in a new Middle East conflagration.

Clearing the Hurdles

Sadat landed at Andrews Air Force base convinced that the parties had arrived at the "crucial crossroads" while close on his heels Begin opined the talks would be "most momentous". Before Carter left the White House for the 95 km. journey to Camp David he warned that compromises would be mandatory for progress. The visiting heads of government were merely cordial towards each other but ostentatiously affectionate towards their American host, immediately enfolding him in bear-hugs at the Catoctin mountains helipad.

With the world's press kept at bay beyond electronically-monitored, barbed-wire fences, the distinguished guests settled into wooden lodges in the heavily-guarded 143 acre compound. The emphasis was to be on informality where antagonists would be eased into leisurely encounters with one another and some of the first pictures to be flashed across the world showed Israel's Defense Minister braking his bicycle ride for a warm reunion with a track-suited Egyptian President. The summit of no fixed duration opened on 6th September 1978 with a joint prayer for peace at the prompting of First Lady Rosalynn Carter. Newsmen closeted in the American Legion Auditorium at the village of Thurmont 11 km. away began thumbsucking copy amid a virtual news blackout. In the sylvan quietude, where U.S. chief executives since Roosevelt had thrown off the cares of state, the politicians and their aides sparred gingerly as they called on each other in cabins built with stone fireplaces and heavy beamed ceilings. The hosts, who had stage-managed the housing of Israelis and Egyptians in alternating lodges to encourage fraternization, infused their unique style of work and leisure. The teams moved from armchairs in "Aspen", the presidential cabin, to Begin's "Birch" lodge and Sadat's "Dogwood" quarters. They talked in motorized golf carts, chatted while playing chess and exchanged ideas on long walks along leafy paths. Dressed casually in sports wear or in the navy blue windbreakers emblazoned with the Camp David insignia, the men who alone could decree war or peace played billiards and tennis, then talked until three or four in the morning, rising again when deer and raccoons began padding the virgin woods at dawn.

Five secluded days later the relaxed leaders broke for a four hour trip to the nearby rolling green fields of Gettysburg, Pennsylvania, giving no hint of any progress. But they could not have failed to be moved by the healing words of Abraham Lincoln, spoken there 115 years earlier, at the dedication of the Civil War battlefield cemetery. " . . . . . that we here highly resolve that these dead shall not have died in vain — that this nation, under God, shall have a new birth of freedom . . . ."

Reminded of the enormity of their charge, the three national leaders returned to their mountaintop retreat. A restless, uninformed press see-sawed with conflicting reports of failure and breakthrough. But spared the spotlight of media publicity, the tieless men of three faiths pressed on in their united quest for peace. Living cheek by jowl for 13 days and nights, the polyglot teams ebbed and flowed in their measure of trust and misunderstanding of each other. There were times, as Begin related later, when difficult moments escalated into crises and hints were dropped that there might be a walkout. But the U.S. President, indefatigably pacifying and catalysing, applied healing balm to cool simmering passions and national pride. Right up until the last hours of a deadline eventually decided upon, Carter huddled with the leaders of the two ancient peoples.

On Sunday evening 17th September they left the rustic cabins and surfaced in the East Room of the White House below the unfurled flags of their countries. When Carter rose and began the formal announcement it surpassed all expectations and left a flabbergasted world gaping with incredulity. Agreement had been reached on a Framework for Peace in the Middle East and on a separate Framework for the conclusion of a Peace Treaty between Egypt and Israel. Begin and Sadat had committed themselves to sign a full peace treaty within three months and to exchange diplomats within a year.

Israel had backed down completely on the Sinai settlements, consenting to a total withdrawal of all military forces and civilians, though this agonizing about face would have to be condoned by the Israeli Knesset within two weeks. A five year transitional period had been agreed upon for the West Bank and Gaza, during which the Israel military government would be withdrawn and a self-governing authority would be elected with autonomous powers.

The American President had won a signal triumph as reconciler and was showered with kudos from both the Egyptian and the Israeli. "It was the Jimmy Carter Conference. The President won the day," Premier Begin exulted before U.S. congressmen and other VIPs seated in the White House. Both he and Sadat locked themselves in embraces and handshakes, agreeing to try and sign the Peace Treaty within two, instead of three months.

All sides were quick to stress that Egypt and Israel were not about to sign a separate treaty but rather a treaty as a first step to a comprehensive peace in the Middle East. Yet the lonely Arab had to endure the wrath of the Arab states and the protest resignation, for the second time in just over a year, of his foreign minister. Begin moved to protect his own flank from right-wing criticism on home ground by stentoriously announcing that Israel would have a presence in certain places in the West Bank forever. While his clamorous critics from the Rafiah and other settlement areas converged on Jerusalem to protest, Begin told impassioned legislators that the choice was painful but clear: if the settlements remained there could be no peace treaty. Left with such a stark choice the parliamentarians endorsed, by a more than two-thirds majority, the Camp David agreements and removal of all settlers from the Sinai.

On 12th October the Israeli and Egyptian foreign and defense ministers met at Blair House, Washington, directly opposite the White House, to flesh out the bones of the peace treaty. But differences sprouted almost immediately. The bargaining was harder than anticipated over clauses that would bind them for generations to come. Fissures became cracks which split wider into chasms as the friendly foes tried to protect their own interests before sealing the fate of posterity. They disagreed on linking the treaty with progress on the fate of the West Bank and Gaza; they fell apart over Egypt's new commitments to Israel and her standing obligations to the Arab world; there were sharp differences over the sale of Sinai oil, on the timing of the exchange of diplomats and on the deployment of troops.

At length the entire peace process was almost skewered by Israel's decision to expand existing settlements in the disputed West Bank area. Only the personal intervention of the U.S. President soothed an irate Sadat from breaking up the Washington talks. So deep was the estrangement that Sadat boycotted what should have been a triumphant ceremony in Oslo, where both he and Begin were to receive the Nobel Peace Prize for 1978. Neither visits by the Israeli and Egyptian Prime Ministers to the U.S., nor a flight by Secretary of State Cyrus Vance to the Middle East could bridge the widening gulf. Only when the strident new fundamentalism of Islam toppled the Shah of Iran in January did a new sense of desperate urgency arise. The threat of Iran's insidious influence on moderate Arab governments gained weight when the U.S. Secretary of Defense jetted into Israel and Egypt to assess the new tilt in the regional balance of power. Snatching at the threads of common purpose, Secretary Vance summoned Foreign Minister Dayan and Premier Mustapha Khalil to four days of a replay of September's seclusion at Camp David. But at its conclusion Israel charged Egypt with taking more extreme positions. Even the goodwill of the past had soured. When Israel rejected a White House invitation for Begin to meet with Khalil in Washington, Carter made a transatlantic last minute plea and Begin flew off for "personal talks" with the President.

The air was charged with foreboding as the spirited Israeli leader touched down at Andrews Air Force base and contemptuously spoke of the "sham document" Israel had been asked to sign. Simultaneously the Egyptian media reverted to labelling Begin a terrorist. No progress was made during the four days he was closeted with the President and advisors. But when, on 4th March, Carter offered new proposals and Israel's cabinet gave them the nod within 24 hours, there was a dramatic turnabout. It was announced that the 39th President of the United States would become the second chief executive in office to visit the Middle East. Carter was once again staking his political credibility on his personal diplomacy, only this time failure would more than demean him personally; it would most likely be the death knell for the entire peace epic because if, having come so far, the parties could not scale the last few rungs, there would be profound disillusionment, a return to ardent nationalism and a beating of war drums.

All ethnic groups wished Prime Minister Begin success before his departure for Camp David.

The accent was on informality at Camp David

Three statesmen seeking a single direction
at the Maryland presidential retreat.
Rosalynn Carter and Aliza Begin relaxing while
their husbands work overtime for peace.

Leisurely appearances masked an intense struggle with fundamental principles and national pride at the presidential retreat in the Catoctin mountains.

Edging closer to agreement, the leaders of Israel and Egypt about to enter the Camp David cabin of President Carter.
(Top) A Presidential kiss for Mrs. Aliza Begin.

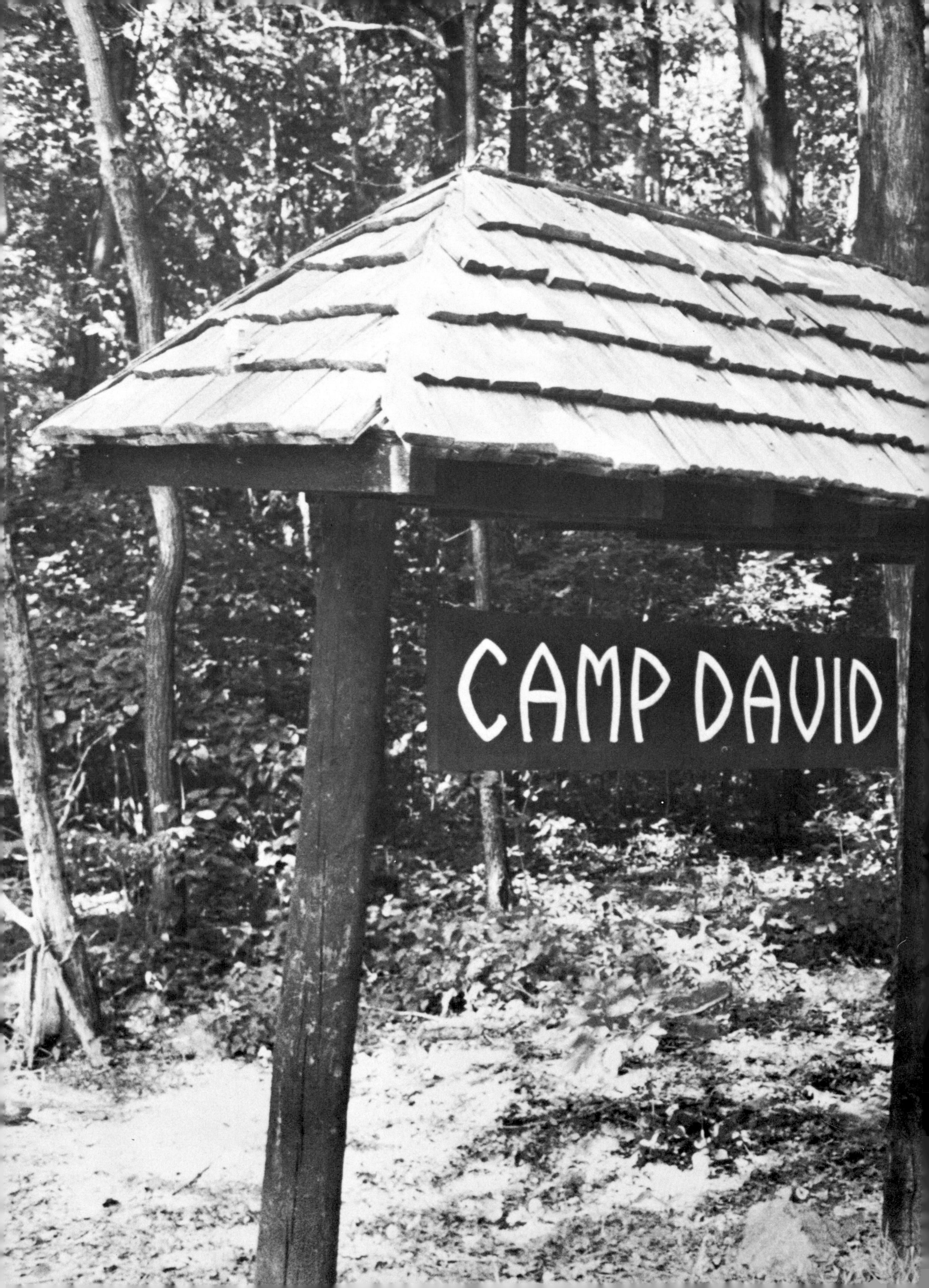
CAMP DAVID

For 13 days and nights they lived cheek by jowl in quest of agreement

**Face to face and man to man
in the Maryland mountains**

**Thirteen days later they surfaced in the
East Room of the White House to announce
agreement at Camp David.**

(Top left) Jimmy & Rosalynn Carter arrive at Ben-Gurion airport in March 1979.
(Right) Rosalynn Carter swept off her feet while visiting a new immigrants' absorption center.
(Below) The Begins host the Carters at a Sabbath dinner

(Above) A kiss from Jimmy Carter for a pretty girl soldier
(Below) The American President visits President Yitzhak Navon at his official residence in Jerusalem

Swords into Plowshares

Tumarkin 79

Even before the silver, blue and white Air Force One streaked across the skies of Cairo, the 39-member Egyptian cabinet was shredding Carter's new proposals. But none of this was known to cheering Cairenes thrilled by the majesty of a presidential cavalcade. The following day Egyptian multitudes came out like swarms of desert locusts to wave as Carter and Sadat whistle-stopped in a dazzling train ride to coastal Alexandria.

Away from the limelight they grappled with the sensitive issues without success. Notwithstanding, Carter stood before the People's Assembly to pay singular tribute to the valiant man who made the first move towards peace. "Sixteen months ago," he recalled, "one man, Anwar el-Sadat, rose up and said 'enough of war, it is time for peace.' " It had all happened so long ago that its very recollection was regarded with nostalgia.

As the American and his entourage prepared to fly on to Israel police raided the Jerusalem headquarters of Gush Emunim. A number of people were taken into protective custody and documents were seized. Apprehension grew as the president drove straight from Ben-Gurion airport to the home of Premier Begin, where an after-dinner tête-à-tête broke up past midnight.

Amid mounting speculation that Egypt had upped the ante, the second incumbent president to visit Israel met in earnest conclave with Begin and the cabinet security committee. The peace process was reportedly still hanging by a thread when Carter's motorcade wound its way to the Knesset through the picturesque Valley of the Cross. Suddenly Gush Emunim fanatics broke through security cordons, zigzagging between cars, but too late to halt the President. When Begin's limousine arrived at the parliament building right-wing opponents, fearing government capitulation to American pressure, shrieked "traitor" and club-swinging police battled with others trying to crash through police barriers. Carter's own arrival was marked by cheers from supporters of the "Peace Now" movement holding flaming torches aloft.

The speeches of both leaders were candid restatements of worn themes and promises of distant prizes. There was no hint of real advancement and Carter discarded his draft speeches of despair and glad tidings in favor of words of concern, caution and hope. Begin somberly referred to differences of opinion. Again they sat, until the pre-dawn hours, vainly trying to whittle away the blocks to peace. With barely a few hours sleep they rose to reason with each other once more. But in the evening Carter as much as admitted stalemate at a

Knesset banquet. Faith alone made him "absolutely confident" that neither Begin nor Sadat would allow "this great opportunity for peace to slip away."

Meanwhile in Egypt regular television broadcasts were interrupted for a flash announcement that Carter would stopover on his flight home the following morning for talks with Sadat at Cairo airport.

The outcome of a breakfast meeting at Jerusalem's King David Hotel between the President, 54, and the Premier, 65, apparently failed for at Ben-Gurion airport Carter spoke of unresolved issues. A nauseous feeling of doom swept the region as the president's plushly-equipped Boeing 707 lifted off into the pewter-colored sky. In his first foray into shuttle diplomacy Carter was going back empty-handed and the identical message was being filed across the world by the pack of newsmen at his heels.

But the Georgian's scheduled one-hour talks with Sadat filtered into two and then three hours. At 5 p.m. Carter spoke for 10 minutes by telephone with the Israeli Premier and shortly afterwards summoned reporters. "I have a statement to make which I consider to be extremely important," said the fatigued American. President Sadat had just accepted identical proposals which Begin would shortly put to his cabinet. When a reporter asked diffidently whether there would be peace if the Israeli cabinet approved, Carter nodded and said "yes". Near pandemonium broke out as the press scattered to file bulletins on the sensational update. The spotlight turned on Israel as Begin broadcast nationwide that the cabinet would meet the following day. If the two outstanding problems could be resolved, the draft treaty would go before the Knesset for endorsement and the historic treaty could be signed just one week away. But if the Knesset gave the thumbs down, Begin promised his government would resign.

Meanwhile at Andrews Air Force base some 1,000 cheering VIPs and others gave Carter a rousing welcome as his plane made a nighttime landing. With the Israel cabinet giving the final litmus test to the crucial clauses, Carter told the airport crowd, "you are looking at a tired but grateful man. The leaders of Egypt and Israel are now daring to break the pattern of 30 years of bitterness and war." Before being whisked off to bed he left instructions to be woken up "if the news (from Israel) is good."

The cabinet wrangled for almost seven hours before it voted to accept what Sadat had already agreed to. A day later the Egyptian cabinet put its own seal on the draft treaty. "I hope the past enmity between the two nations will be something of a memory," declared Prime Minister Khalil.

On 20th March Israel's parliamentarians left their farms and offices for Jerusalem. As they filed in for the momentous session each one picked up two thick volumes. One was 52 pages of English, the other 30 sheets of Hebrew. They bore the same title: "A Treaty of Peace between the Arab Republic of Egypt and the State of Israel". Through two days and a night of often acrimonious and disorderly conduct, they rose, one after the other, to state their hopes, their fears and their convictions. At 4.30 a.m. on 22nd March the weary men and women who had blotted out every other program on Israel television, slouched in for the balloting. The final tally was 95 in favor, 18 against, two abstentions and five absentees.

"Marvelous," exclaimed Sadat on hearing the news.

"It is a voice heard around the world," said a relieved Carter.

A little more than 100 hours later, on 26th March 1979, three men walked up a raised dais on the north lawn of the White House to a standing ovation from some 1,500 distinguished invitees as millions more sat before TV screens in a worldwide hook-up. A band struck up the national anthems of the three countries while the trio stood with backs to the Ionic columns of the executive mansion. Then Carter, flanked by his allies for peace, sat down to sign the historic blue leather-bound documents printed in English, Arabic and Hebrew. One sentence from the mass of print summed it all up: "The state of war between the parties will be terminated and peace will be established between them . . . . ."

"Let's have a handshake," suggested the U.S. President when the formalities were over. And as they rose for the triple clasp the Baptist turned to the Moslem and the Jew. "I'm so proud of both of you," he said.

For Jimmy Carter, who was the first to make a speech, it was a time to feel proud. He had, within two years of his advent as a novice onto the world stage, saved the saga from congealing into failure.

"Today we celebrate a victory, not of a bloody military campaign but of an inspiring peace campaign," he said. Carter heaped laurels on both Sadat and Begin who had been able to lead their wavering nations by sheer force of character and immense stature. "Two leaders who will loom large in the history of nations — Anwar el-Sadat and Menachem Begin — have conducted this campaign with all the courage, tenacity, brilliance and inspiration of any generals who ever led men and machines onto the field of battle." To the gathering forces of Arabism and communism opposed to the treaty, Carter warned, "let those who would shatter peace, who would callously spill more blood, be aware that we will wage peace." He upheld the treaty as an inspiration to other peoples joined in battle: "Let history record that deep, ancient antagonisms can be settled without bloodshed, waste of life and destruction of land. Let us now reward all the children of Abraham who hunger for a comprehensive peace in the Middle East."

Then the slim man from the Nile Delta took the microphone. "Today a new dawn is emerging out of the darkness of the past. Let there be no more wars and bloodshed between Arabs and Israelis." Drawing on the words of the Hebrew prophet Isaiah to express a universal aspiration, he continued, "let us work together until the day comes when they beat their swords into plowshares and their spears into pruning hooks." His estimation of the American President bordered on adulation. "The man who performed the miracle was Jimmy Carter. There were certain moments when hope was eroding and retreating in the face of crisis. However, President Carter remained unshaken in his confidence and determination."

Begin, citing the same verse from Isaiah, said the vision of beating swords into plowshares should never be forsaken, despite the tragedies and disappointments of the past. He, too, had encomiums for Carter's "labors which have borne blessed fruit." Turning to his erstwhile enemy, Begin continued: "President Sadat is a hero because he showed great civil courage in the face of adversity. Sometimes civil courage is more notable than military courage." Then the Israeli faced his global audience to pledge "No more bloodshed! No more war! No more bereavement!" Finally, placing a kipa (skullcap) on his head, the man who led the nation of modern Israel recited the Hebrew text of Psalm 126, penned in the days of ancient Israel.

The ceremony was over. It had lasted the scheduled hour and the men who had roller-coasted towards peace now savored the moment of its attainment. There were embraces and kisses, handshakes and backslapping. Sixteen months ago a gauntlet had been flung down in the name of peace. Now all people of goodwill were at one in the dawn of a new era. Animosities of the past had given way to the challenges of the future. Isaiah's yearning cry had echoed down the centuries and been answered in the lands of the psalmists and the Pharaohs.

All smiles after the signing of the historic Peace Treaty on the north lawn of the White House, 26th March 1979

American acclaim for Israeli Prime Minister Menachem Begin

With the Peace Treaty signed, three statesmen rise to share the plaudits

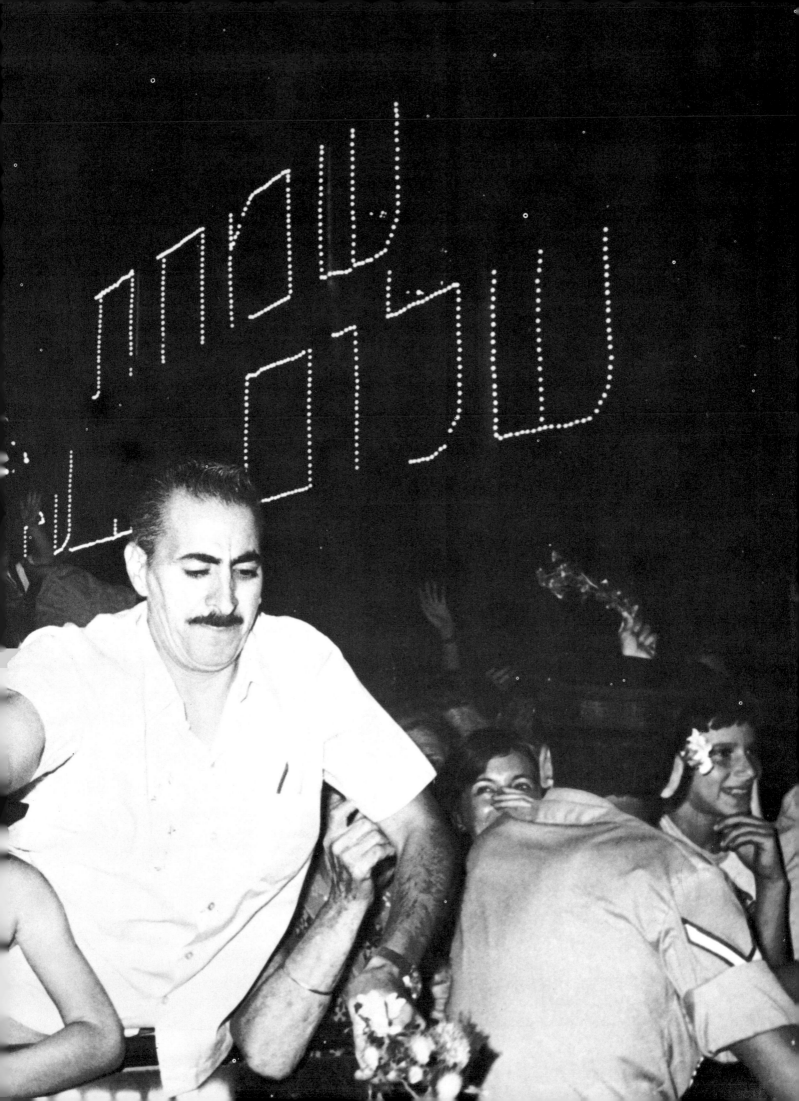

Millions around the world watched the live TV spectacular from the north lawn of the White House

A time to congratulate each other

Standing to attention in honor of each other's national anthem. (Inset) President Sadat shakes Premier Begin's hand after the Israeli had recited Psalm 126

(Above) St. Catherine's Monastery in th Sinai desert, within walking distance of Mt. Sinai, atop whic Anwar Sadat said he would one day build triple shrines fo Moslems, Jews and Christians. (Below) Men of three faiths achieve a unite goal of peace

Erstwhile foes embrace in peace as the President of the U.S. applauds the start of a new era

Jimmy Carter hosts dinner guests Mrs. Jihan Sadat and Menachem Begin at a White House celebration

Signing the Peace Treaty

A triple clasp after the signing

Toasting the peace

Swords into plowshares and spears into pruning hooks

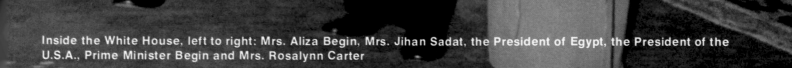

Inside the White House, left to right: Mrs. Aliza Begin, Mrs. Jihan Sadat, the President of Egypt, the President of the U.S.A., Prime Minister Begin and Mrs. Rosalynn Carter

After 30 years of war a new generation would be raised in peace

Opposite: Blessed be the peacemakers

A time to laugh and a time to dance

An affectionate embrace for Amy Carter from an Israeli grandfather

(Above left) Jihan Sadat gets a helping hand from Menachem Begin
(Above right) Aliza Begin and Rosalynn Carter at the White House
(Below) A triumphant welcome home

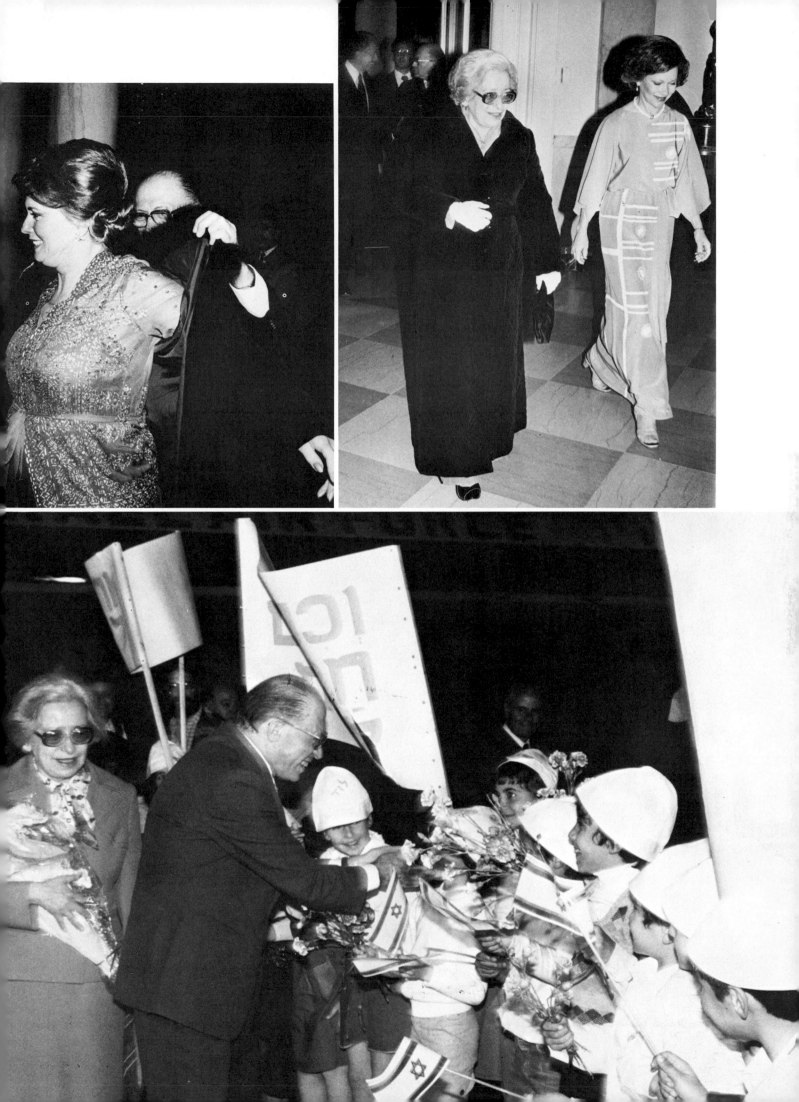

For everything there is a season, and a time for every matter under heaven; a time for war, and a time for peace.

A time to weep, and a time to laugh.

Close personal friendships evolved on the road to peace

Shalom, Peace, Salaam

THE WASHINGTON HILTON

" I have come from the land of Israel, the land of Zion and
Jerusalem, and here I am, in humility and with pride, as a son
of the Jewish people, as one of the generation of the Holocaust and Redemption.
The ancient Jewish people gave the world the vision of eternal peace,
of universal disarmament, of abolishing the teaching and learning of war. Two
prophets, Yeshayahu Ben Amotz and Micha Hamorashti, having foreseen
the spiritual unity of man under God — with His word coming forth
from Jerusalem — gave the nations of the world the following vision expressed
in identical terms:

" And they shall beat their swords into ploughshares and their
spears into pruning hooks. Nation shall not lift up sword against nation;
neither shall they learn war any more."

Despite the tragedies and disappointments of the past we must never
forsake that vision, that human dream, that unshakable faith...

Connecticut Avenue at Columbia Road, N.W.   Washington, D.C. 20009   202/483-3000

                    great
It is a ~~great~~ day in your life, dear President of the United States. You have worked so hard, so insistently, so consistently, for this goal; and your labors and your devotion have God-blessed joined. ~~President~~ Our friend, President Sadat ~~said~~ said that you are the "unknown soldier" of the peace-making effort. I agree, but still, as usually, with ~~and~~ an amendment. A soldier in the service of peace you are, you are, dear President, even, horrible dictu, an _intransigeant fighter_ for peace, but but ~~President~~ Jimmy Carter, the President of the United States is not completely unknown. And so is his effort, which will be remembered by generations to come.

It is, of course, a good day in your life, dear President of the Arab Republic of Egypt. In the face of adversity and hostility you have
                            the human
demonstrated ~~that~~ value that can change history; civil courage. A great field-commander once said: civil courage is sometimes more difficult to show than military courage. You showed both. But now it is time for all of us, to show _civil_ courage in order to proclaim to our peoples, and to others: no more war, no more bloodshed

no more bloodshed — peace unto you, ֿֿֿֿֿ shalom, salaam — for ever...

But it is, ladies and gentlemen, the third greatest day in my life. The first was day 14th 1948 when our flag was hoisted, our independence in our ancestors' land was proclaimed, after 1878 years of dispersion, persecution, and physical destruction. 'We fought for our liberation — and won the day. That was spring; such a spring we can never have again.

The second day was when Jerusalem became our city, and our brave, perhaps most hardened soldiers, the parachutists, embraced with tears and kissed the ancient stones of the remnants of the wall destined to protect the chosen place of God's glory. Our hearts wept with them — in remembrance.

ירושלים בניתה פעולנו שלהם באנו ומהם לו עיניו

This is the third day in my life. I have signed a treaty of peace, with our neighbours, with Egypt...

שיר המעלות, בשוב ה' את שיבת ציון, היינו כחולמים

אז ימלא שחוק פינו ולשוננו רנה; אז יאמרו בגוים:

הגדיל ה' לעשות עם אלה. הגדיל ה' לעשות עמנו, היינו שמחים.

שובה ה' את שבותנו, שובה ה' את שבותנו, כאפיקים בנגב.

הזורעים בדמעה, ברנה יקצורו. הזורעים בדמעה, ברנה יקצורו

הלוך ילך ובכה נושא משך הזרע, בוא יבוא ברנה נושא אלומותיו.

בוא יבוא ברנה נושא אלומותיו.

their name, although they cried out: save us, save us, [illegible] de profundis, from the depths of the pit and agony; that is the song of degrees written two millenia and five hundred years ago when our forefathers returned from their first exile to Jerusalem, to Zion:

I will not translate. Every man, whether Jew or Christian or Muslim, can read it in his own language. It is just Psalm one hundred twenty six.

A red carpet welcome, with an honor guard and a bouquet of flowers from a child, during Premier Begin's visit to Egypt.

Vice-President Hosni Mubarek accompanies Prime Minister Begin past an honor guard after a momentous touchdown on Egyptian soil. (Inset) Israeli journalists disembarking in Egypt from an Israeli plane marked with the words Salaam and Shalom.

The Egyptian who broke the ice in Jerusalem now hosts the Israeli Premier in the Egyptian capital.

No longer a dream, Prime Minister Begin exults during a tour of the pyramids.

A new era is ushered in for Premier Begin and his countrymen as they explore the glories of ancient Egypt and meet their new allies for peace.

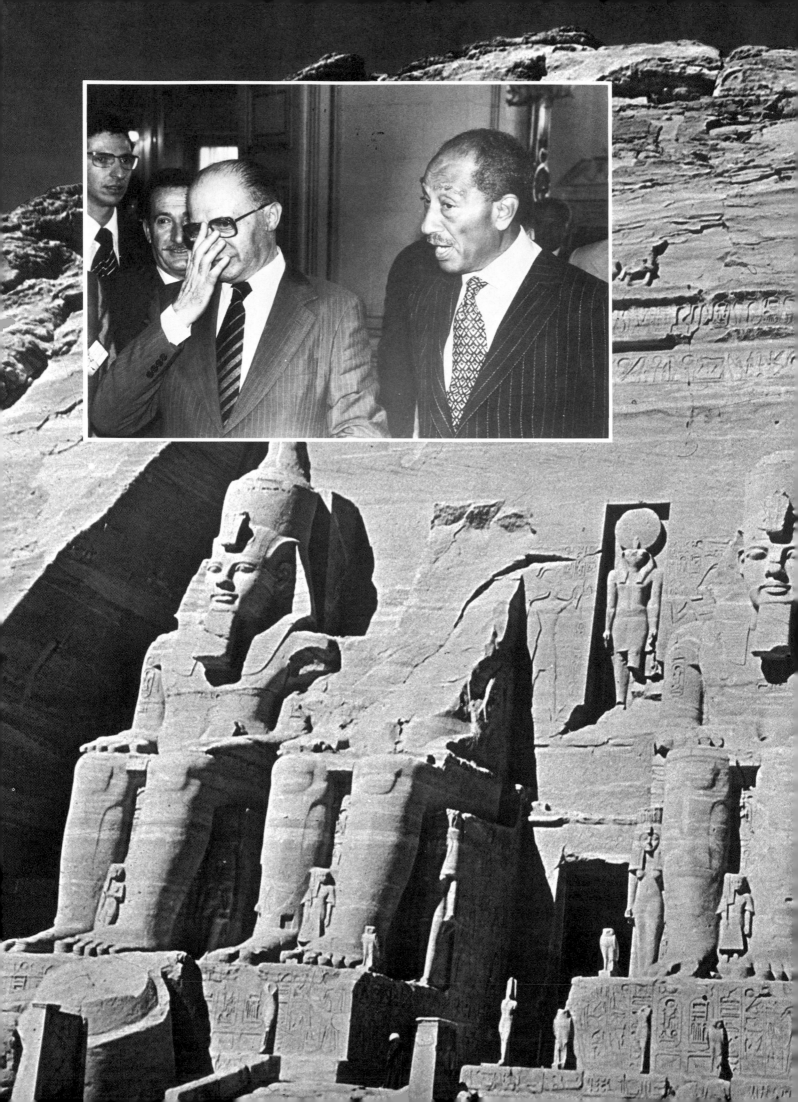

Reaping the Rewards

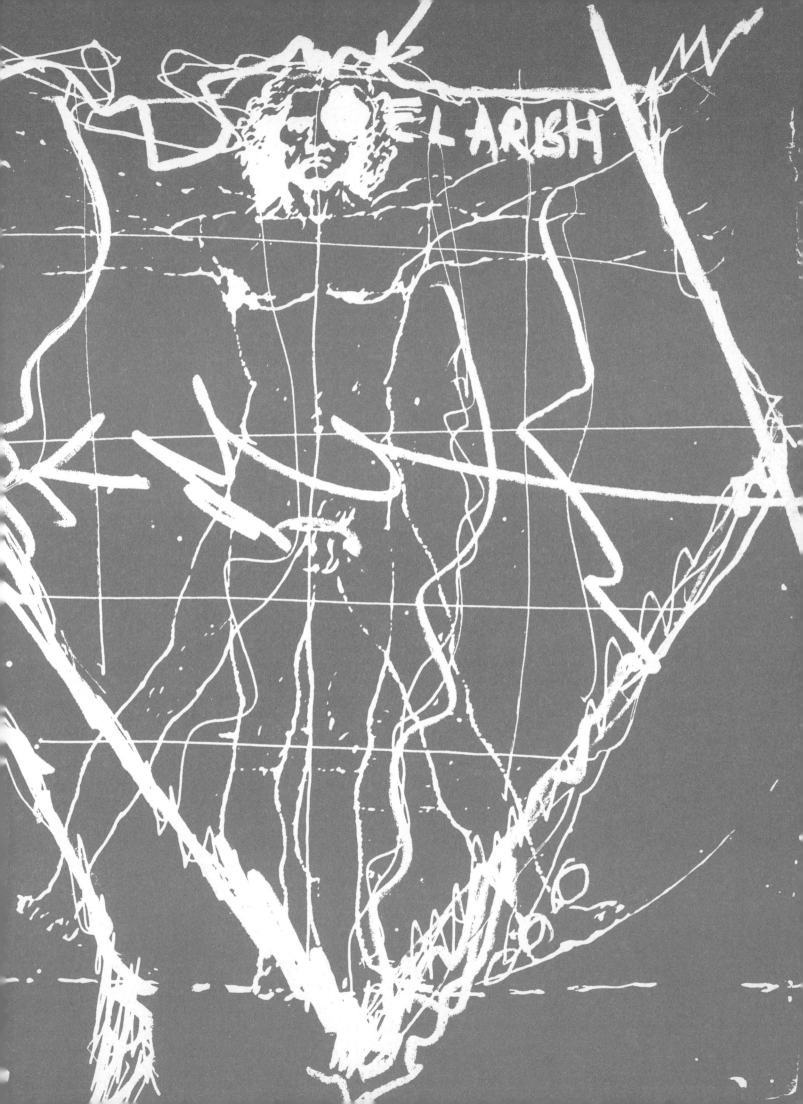

Four days in May 1979 silenced the cynics as the epoch-making
Peace Treaty bore its first fruits. In these 96 hours Israel formally
handed back the Sinai capital of El Arish to Egypt, the borders were
flung open symbolically, disabled war veterans from both armies met to
fraternize, some 100,000 citizens of Beer Sheva lined their streets to
cheer the visiting Egyptian President, and Israeli warships made history
by sailing through the Suez Canal.

The transfer of El Arish and an almost 100 kilometer coastal strip was
made eight months before the time stipulated in the Peace Treaty. It
was a vivid expression of Israel's intention to normalize relations with
her western neighbor. Israel's dozen years of administering the
Mediterranean coastal town came to an end on Friday 25th May during
a parade ground ceremony in front of the main Israeli military canteen
in the Sinai. As the blue Star of David on a white background was
lowered slowly, white and blue uniformed Egyptian soldiers and
khaki-clad Israeli troops with white military police headgear stiffly
presented arms. Officers of both nations saluted smartly while the
Israeli national anthem was played. Said Major-General Dan Shomron,
officer commanding southern command, in his order of the day: "The
handing over of El Arish today is the clearest and most sincere
expression of our desire for peace." Minutes later the black, white and
red Egyptian flag was aloft and the 45,000 El Arishis were cheering
themselves hoarse.

The following day the beribboned President of Egypt, in the white
uniform of an admiral, stood before a flag pole in the center of the
town. With military precision four officers from his armed services
advanced to offer him their nation's flag. Sadat bowed reverently to
kiss it then placed the colored cloth across his outstretched arms as
dozens of war veterans, officers and townspeople leaned forward to
press their lips to it. Sadat then hoisted it himself, flanked by his
vice-president and defense minister. A 15-gun salute boomed across
the town, pigeons scattered and colored balloons drifted up into the
clear desert skies. El Arish, conquered by a swift thrust of the Israel
Defense Forces during the Six Day War and transferred to Egyptian
military government 24 hours earlier, now passed over to local civilian
authorities. A nation's flag again flew over its land — thanks to a wise
Arab leader and a militarily courageous people who had accepted the
sincerity behind a proffered olive branch.

On Sunday 27th May Menachem Begin joined Sadat for summit talks
at a refurbished presidential resthouse close to El Arish's fine-grained
sandy beach shaded by thousands of slender palm trees. They arrived

at a momentous decision but kept it secret until after entering the cinema hall of the former Israeli military government. Inside were 85 disabled war veterans who had clashed with each other in the desert sands. Some were blind, others sat in wheelchairs, a few had stumps of amputated limbs and several bore the scars of burns. Many of them wept when the Israeli leader announced, "the President and I proclaim that the borders of Egypt and Israel are open. The people of Egypt will be able to visit Israel and the people of Israel will be able to visit Egypt."

Eighteen days later the first Israeli passport holder sailed from Tel Aviv's marina direct to Port Said and was welcomed graciously and with warm hospitality. Cross-pollination of ideas, cultures and perspectives had begun. The politicians had done their work in ending the state of war and designing a pattern for the future. Now the public would weave the threads of everyday contact.

From El Arish the statesmen helicoptered to the Negev desert capital of Beer Sheva, where their common biblical patriarch, Abraham, had pitched his tent and watered his flocks. The mass outpouring of public esteem for Sadat was evident from the tens of thousands of Israelis who cheered the Egyptian as he drove through streets decked with the flags of both countries and strung with banners proclaiming "The City of Abraham welcomes Anwar Sadat". They were in festive mood and entertainment troupes sang of peace, shalom and salaam. In a gesture of respect, both President Yitzhak Navon and Mayor Eliahu Nawi addressed the multitudes in the mother tongue of the visiting Arab. When he rose to reply the honored guest spoke in English. "There will be no more barriers between our peoples," he said, "no more anxiety or insecurity, no more suffering or suspicion."

They drove from the municipality to the ultra-modern architectural façades of Ben-Gurion University of the Negev, where both Begin and Sadat eyed the future. Said the Egyptian head of state: "Fanaticism and self-righteousness are no answer to the complex problems of today. The answer is tolerance, compassion and magnanimity. We will be judged not by the hard positions we took but by the wounds we heal, the souls we saved and the suffering we eliminated." Declared the Israeli head of government: "With God's help, the Middle East, the cradle of human civilization, will again become the source of human progress."

The path to normalizing relations between the two states after a 30-year state of war could not but be paved with drama. When Sadat and Begin boarded the Egyptian's presidential Boeing 737 for a 45

minute symbolic flight over the Sinai desert to open the borders, Sadat told newsmen, "we have agreed on the principle that whenever we can give the peace process a momentum, we shall do it."
He personally was determined to make good his pledge and to show visible intent of goodwill. On Monday 28th May he stupefied the crews of three Israel Navy tank landing craft making the first passage by Israeli warships through the Suez Canal when he appeared on the terrace of his Ismailiya villa to salute and wave at them. The gesture resolved all doubts among the Jewish sailors who had been debating the sincerity behind Sadat's peaceful intentions. To a man, they cheered and waved back. It was, as the biblical preacher wrote, "A time to heal and a time to build up; a time to laugh and a time to dance; a time to love and a time for peace."

Egyptian soldier shakes the hand of Israeli girl soldier shortly before the transfer of El Arish to Egyptian administration

In the dress whites of an admiral, President Sadat salutes the Egyptian flag, while flanked by his vice-president, right, and defense minister, left, at ceremonies in the Sinai capital of El Arish (inset).

Premier Begin bows his head before Egyptian honor guard after transfer of El Arish

(Top) Israeli and Egyptian civil servants express delight at reunion in El Arish as the Sinai capital (below) sprouts banners and boards hailing Anwar Sadat and Peace.

President Sadat holds the Egyptian tricolor before hoisting it at El Arish on Saturday, 26th May 1979.
(Top right) Ecstatic citizens of El Arish celebrate their return to Egyptian rule.
(Center) An honor guard for the Egyptian President
(Bottom) Disabled war veterans about to kiss the Egyptian flag held by Anwar Sadat

Beer Sheva Mayor Eliahu Nawi at the microphone during the ceremony conferring the Freedom of the City on President Sadat

באר־שבע

بئر السبع

BEER-SHEVA

Opposite (Top) Anwar Sadat speaks at Ben-Gurion University of the Negev.
(Center) Israeli Defense Minister Ezer Weizman (left) and leader of the Israel delegation at the talks on autonomy for the West Bank and Gaza, Dr. Yosef Burg (right)
(Bottom) Egyptian Premier Dr. Mustapha Khalil in conversation with Dr. Burg.

(Top) El Arish reverts to Egyptian rule
(Bottom) Sunday, 27th May 1979: President Sadat and Premier Begin symbolically open the borders between their countries with a flight over the Sinai desert

Delegations from the United States, Israel and Egypt assembled at Ben-Gurion University of the Negev at Beer Sheva on Friday, 25th May 1979 for the opening of talks on autonomy for the West Bank and the Gaza Strip.

After 12 years of Israeli occupation, the northern Sinai town of El Arish reverts to Egyptian rule in colorful ceremonies

ַ... נַעֲשָׂה בְּוַשִׁינגטון, דִי סִי בְּיוֹם זֶה, כ"ז בַּאֲדָר לִשְׁנַת תשל"ט, 26 בְּמַרץ 1979.
... עִבְרִית נְסוּחָה בג' רִיּח, הָעִברִית וְהָאַנגלִית וְכָל נוֹסַח אָמִין נֶחֶזְדָה שָׁוֶה.
... אֵי וְגִדּוּלֵי פֵּשֶר, יַכְרִיעַ רְנוֹטֵח הָאַנגלִי.

حِرِّرَ فِي وَاشِنطُن دِي سِي فِي ٢٦ مارِس ١٩٧٩م و٢٧ رِبِيعِ الأول ١٣٩٩هـ
مِن ثَلاثٍ نُسَخ بِاللُّغَاتِ العِبرِية والعَرَبِيَّة والاِنجلِيزِيَّة وتُعتَبَر جَمِيعُها مُتَسَاوِيَة
الحُجِّيَّة، وفِي حَالةِ الخِلافِ حَولَ التَّفسِيرِ فَيَكُون النَّصُّ الاِنجلِيزِي هُوَ الذِي يُعتَدُّ بِهِ.

DONE at Washington, D.C. this 26th day of March, 1979, in
triplicate in the Hebrew, Arabic, and English languages, each
text being equally authentic. In case of any divergence of
interpretation, the English text shall prevail.

בְּשֵׁם מֶמְשֶׁלֶת יִשְׂרָאֵל :

בשם ממשלת הרפובליקה הערבית
של מצרים :

مِن حُكُومَة
اسرائيـــــل :

مِن حُكُومَة
جُمهُورِيَّة مِصر العَرَبِيَّة :

For the Government
of Israel:

For the Government of the
Arab Republic of Egypt:

הוֹעַד עַל-יְדֵי :

شَهِدَ التَّوقِيع :

Witnessed by:

גַ'ימִי קַארטֶר, נָשִׂיא
אַרצוֹת הַבְּרִית שֶׁל אַמֶרִיקָה

جِيمِي كارتِر، رَئِيس
الوِلايَاتِ المُتَّحِدَةِ الأمرِيكِيَّة

Jimmy Carter, President
of the United States of America